# THE BACCHAE

Other works from Serpent Club Press:

2013
*Moon on Water*
Matthew Gasda

2014
*Autumn, Again; Spring, Anew*
Michael Skelton and Stephen Morel

*On Bicycling: An Introduction*
Samuel Atticus Steffen

2015
*Sonata for Piano and Violin*
Matthew Gasda

*New Writing: Volume 1*
A Compilation

*Circumambulate*
Daniel Bossert

# THE

# BACCHAE

## An adaptation
### By Matthew Gasda

"Frazer's account of the magical and religious views of mankind is unsatisfactory; it makes these views look like errors."

– Wittgenstein

THE BACCHAE
Copyright © Serpent Club Press, 2015
All rights reserved

Serpent Club Press books may be purchased for educational, business, or sales
promotional use. For more information please contact Serpent Club Press at
theserpentclub@gmail.com

First Edition

Printed in the United States of America
Set in Williams Caslon
Designed by Emily Gasda

ISBN
9780990664369

LCCN
2015916533

*The Bacchae* by Matthew Gasda was commissioned and developed by and for the world premier performance with the State University of New York, Oswego Theatre Department in 2015. Jessica Hester, dramaturg.

## Dramatis Personae

*In order of appearance:*

DIONYSUS, the God in human form. He is worshipped by the Bacchae.

Chorus called THE RAVING ONES, made up of a number of actors, speaks throughout the play in various numbers of those actors (sometimes all, sometimes few or one), but always moves as one. They play the voice of the world in a way, and they also play and appear to be the Bacchae of the title, Dionysus's female followers. They move gracefully in a coordinated way.

Chorus called GHOST, made up of a number of actors, speaks throughout the play in various numbers of those actors (sometimes all, sometimes few or one), but always moves as one. They play the voice of history in a way, and they also play and appear to be the Bacchae of the title, Dionysus's female followers. They move gracefully in a coordinated way. Ghost contains the chorus member who becomes or turns out to be the character of Agave—who is one of the Bacchae.

TIRESIAS, once a prophet, now an old counselor and companion to Cadmus.

CADMUS, Pentheus's father, once king of Thebes and a legendary character in his youth.

PENTHEUS, the young current king of Thebes, Cadmus's son. A military man.

HEIMON, a soldier and retainer of Pentheus's. "Heimon" means "blood" in Ancient Greek.

ACTEON, a soldier and retainer of Pentheus's. "Acteon" is a reference to the Ancient Greek legend of the hunter killed by his own dogs.

LYKOS, a humble shepherd.

AGAVE, mother of Pentheus.


*The characters are gendered. The actors playing them may or may not share their character's gender. Either way, they should be able to play their essences.*

Matthew Gasda's *The Bacchae* was first performed by the SUNY Oswego Theater Department in October 2015. Directed by Christopher Carter Sanderson, with Caren Celine Morris as stage manager, Spencer Ventresca as assistant director, Megan Twamley as assistant stage manager, and the following cast:

DIONYSUS
  Nick Cocks
PENTHEUS
  Khari Constantine
CAMDUS
  Max Fehr
TIRESIAS
  Wyatt Gilbert
ACTEON
  Michael Calobrisi
HEIMON
  Matt McCabe
LYKOS
  Iury Esquarcio
AGAVE/GHOST CHORUS LEADER
  Alyssa Scruton
GHOST CHORUS, UNDERSTUDY TIRESIAS
  Emma Johnson
GHOST CHORUS, UNDERSTUDY CADMUS
  Remington
GHOST CHORUS, UNDERSTUDY HEIMON
  Robert O'Leary
GHOST CHORUS, UNDERSTUDY AGAVE
  Samantha Keeney

GHOST CHORUS
    Elsa Neider
RAVING ONES CHORUS LEADER/
    UNDERSTUDY DIONYSUS
    Anna Richardson
RAVING ONES CHORUS, UNDERSTUDY
    PENTHEUS
    Libbie Wansink
RAVING ONES CHORUS, UNDERSTUDY LYKOS
    Emily Stott
RAVING ONES CHORUS, UNDERSTUDY GHOST
    CHORUS LEADER
    Alex Matsu
RAVING ONES CHORUS, UNDERSTUDY RAVING
    ONES CHORUS LEADER
    Kelci Schlierf
UNDERSTUDY ACTEON, GHOSTS CHORUS/
    UNDERSTUDY
    Spencer Ventresca

# Prologue

*Enter Dionysus.*

Dionysus

And simultaneously, I am constructed at birth and death into the spirit I understand myself to be; Dionysus: and moving inwards from those two points I reach a perpetual present which grows through the fence of consciousness like a rose: the scent of which permeates, and becomes part of me; because my body is constructed so that it may shed itself of itself until all that is left is the unspeakable, subjective aspect of time. So my elegies blossom into flowers. So it is a wonderful and desolate thing to be the middle link in a chain that is broken. Like the wings I am trying to construct from metaphor: the wings I made up to re-enchant the world. Love without memory. Memory without time. Physical space and spoken language permeate each other like two rivers merging at the mouth of a bay; so this, the desperately forlorn sentence, is the only form of salvation left to me and the translation of self into fiction is the only undeniable magic left in the world. And so I begin nowhere, in the middle of a sentence, in the suspended clause between the creation of new universes and orders of time. My ambiguous language converges and diverges; overlaps; crisscrosses, loops around and doubles back: it echos in conjunction with your pain, complex and sensuously textured. It is the geometry that language takes when it must withstand the ever-increasing pressure of passing time; the erasure of memory; the forgoing of sacrifice. Once, you knew me, but now I am nobody: a stranger, a gift, a secret. Scar tissue has formed around the place where I was remembered in you. My mysteries have been dislocated from the human heart: the birth of the stars, the ritual of mortality. These are the bones of the sacred: a voice, a chord, a form—the presence which traces the arc of lost, or passing, time. Tragedy is my song, and it is for you: it is human, like you are, and it understands what you cannot understand about yourself. And even though you do not recognize them, and their meaning, my Raving Ones still dance for you, they gesture like galaxies which have spent the last of their dark material. You cannot bring them back, my Bacchae, my Raving Ones, even though they come from you and are a part of you. They project back to you everything that you fear: every movement that cuts against the order within. Listen: the stage is not open to reason, the stage enchants itself with what reason does not recognize: it is the nerve-center where fear clusters and is discharged into the air like thunder. I am human and divine. I am the violent rupture of love from the seed of time. My Bacchae follow the logic of this paradox when they dance: they are like bees, who speak when they tremble in the air. Listen to them: they will tell you who you are.

*Enter Raving Ones and Ghost.*

Raving Ones
We have been hollowed out like trees by lightning. When Zeus cast Semele, dying, back to earth, we came to life. Now we are wanderers in the evening: alert to the delicate light of our God.

Ghost
He died. We tore at his body.

Raving Ones
Sweet in the mountains. Milkwhite. Fawnskin. O. Our adoration.

Ghost
O, flute. Ghost.

Raving Ones
The Bacchants stir like butterflies.

Ghost
Time grows tangled with itself, like hair.

Raving Ones
Dancing and singing. Entranced. Sealed and borne from darkness. Him.

Ghost
Purified.

Raving Ones
The loom and shuttle. The weaving of our hands.

Ghost
  My son, we were possessed. Forgive us.

Raving Ones
  Purified.

Ghost
  It was your body that I tore, consumed, loved.

Raving Ones
  No. No longer a nightingale that sings like someone
  in love. Dionysus.

Ghost
  It was your body. The wilderness around the heart.

Raving Ones
  No.

Ghost
  The blue pieces of his eyes.

Raving Ones
  It speaks. The ground speaks. The sun speaks.

Ghost
  Carelessly.

Raving Ones
  Unforced. This love. This touch.

Ghost
  Made lovely by decay: his voice—

Raving Ones

Elusive and indeterminate—incarnated within.

Ghost

He is forever separate from me, silent and gray, muted in his thin immaterial cloth, slowly seeping into the background, no longer discernible from the objects in the world.

Raving Ones

Like the waves the tide pulling us towards you. No. All that is human in us: we give to you, Bacchus. A pot of wine among flowers.

Ghost

Kneeling at the river Mnemosyne, which runs dark with blood; or on the east bank of the Nile, unable to cross; fishing fragments from the river.

# SCENE 1

*Enter Tiresias, approaching the palace, dressed in a Dionysiac costume.*

Tiresias

Is anyone within? Tell the old king that a friend is here.

*Enter Cadmus from within, slowly.*

Cadmus

Thebes is asleep. We are inside its dream.

Tiresias

Do you know why I'm dressed this way?

Cadmus

No.

Tiresias

Because I am trying to wake the city up.

Cadmus

I will join you then. We are not too old to dance, Tiresias.

Tiresias

Or to die.

Cadmus

The God did not distinguish who may dance for him, young or old.

Tiresias

I do not remember what the God said.

Cadmus

Neither do I.

Tiresias

But still, I know the sound of his voice. I know how the ritual proceeds.

Cadmus

Ah. His voice. Yes. My daughter was his mother.

Tiresias

His birth destroyed her.

Cadmus

And joy left me like a bird from its nest.

Tiresias

Why do you want to dance then?

Cadmus

Dancing is the inheritance of death.

> *Enter Pentheus and soldiers on the other side of the stage, dressed as if returning from a military expedition.*

Pentheus

There is a shadow over Thebes, like nightfall in the mountains. Our women, my mother among them, have left to serve the pretender God.

Heimon
  Dionysus—

Pentheus
  They slink away to fuck like animals.

Acteon
  Under the pretext of devotion—

Pentheus
  So we'll hunt them like animals, with iron and smoke.

Ghost
  It was you. It was you we destroyed.

Raving Ones
  Blasphemer.

Heimon
  There is a priest who goads them to follow the God
  of the vine.

Pentheus
  Find him. We will throw him into prison.

Ghost
  You disgraced your house.

    *Exit Soldiers.*

    *Cadmus and Tiresias approach.*

Pentheus
  Even the old men are stained with this mad divinity.

Tiresias
  We are old enough to recognize a new God.

Pentheus
  You and my grandfather look ridiculous.

Cadmus
  Because we are humble.

Pentheus
  Spotted fawn-skins—

Tiresias
  This is what the God wants.

Pentheus
  I want justice, order, reason—

Cadmus
  Intoxication is divine reason.

Pentheus
  It's just terror—

Tiresias
  Terror is a stage you must pass through. On the other
  side, the alien voice is less harsh: it sings.

Pentheus
  No, the voice will destroy us...

Tiresias
  Each day Fate arrives like a messenger whose message

is always the same. You must be astonished by what is beyond you.

Pentheus

A king should never be astonished.

Cadmus

My poor boy...

Pentheus

I put my ear to the earth, and I do not hear anything. But I see a city that wants order—

Cadmus

I would dance like a fool rather than war against a God.

Pentheus

The priests would have us shatter our strength and live like animals in the wild: unprotected, scattered, dumb with fear.

Cadmus

They would restore us to the sanctuary of faith.

Pentheus

This is why you are no longer the King—

Cadmus

I was too impatient for old age...this city will grieve.

Tiresias

I think it is snowing in the universe...

Pentheus

I will have the priest of Dionysus arrested. My soldiers will hunt him like a stray dog.

Ghost

No.

Pentheus

I will bring the Bacchae back within the walls. I will emancipate our women from the ritual of degradation.

Raving Ones

We are nowhere. We are wind.

Cadmus

My child—

Pentheus

No! Do not touch me!

Tiresias

We will pray for you Pentheus. We will pray that you repent.

Cadmus

No human being—me, you—can understand how these things, beauty and terror, life and death, can coexist, can exist in the same world. You must reconcile yourself—

Ghost

White body. Like lightning. O my beautiful. O my spirit.

Pentheus
  I am not afraid of my own power—

Tiresias
  Power is not a human thing—

Pentheus
  Power is the law—

Cadmus
  Boy, take shelter inside a prayer.

Tiresias
  A prayer is a house stronger than Thebes.

Pentheus
  I am the king—

Cadmus
  The king of a certain place: the Gods rule in the wide
  cosmos.

Raving Ones
  Guard all that is in flower. Cut away whatever shows
  decay.

Pentheus
  The Bacchae fly from the human; they are like birds
  who migrate out of season.

Cadmus
  They have a simple ache for nature.

**Pentheus**
My mother's place is here—

**Cadmus**
She has stripped herself to the skin of feeling. I will
follow my daughter in this, and not her son.

**Tiresias**
The scream of the octave flute—

**Pentheus**
Ignore it.

**Cadmus**
That is the God's instrument.

**Ghost**
Floating lights.

**Raving Ones**
River of smoke.

**Tiresias**
The scream again—

**Pentheus**
Ignore it!

**Tiresias**
Pentheus, do you know why man must sacrifice
animals to the Gods?

**Pentheus**
No—

Tiresias
To erase the memory of the time when he was prey and not predator; to erase the guilt of the creature that consumes another's flesh.

Pentheus
What guilt? What memory?

Tiresias
The guilt of having assumed the right to rule over life and death as a God would.

Pentheus
I inherited this crown—

Tiresias
But who did you inherit it from?

Pentheus
Him, Cadmus.

Cadmus
And who did I inherit that crown from?

Pentheus
From...no one.

Cadmus
Are you afraid of what will happen if you join the dancers?

Pentheus
There is no joining them—

Cadmus

Our woman steal into the hills, one by one. Soon, you will be king of an empty house, Pentheus.

Pentheus

You would let your house be disavowed, foreclosed upon, sacrificed, humiliated by them? Your daughters? Your serving girls? Your outright slaves?

Cadmus

I would have what the God would have.

Pentheus

Has the priest of Dionysus tricked you all with his laughter?

Cadmus

We should honor his priests: Dionysus would bless Thebes.

Pentheus

I do not desire his blessing.

Ghost

Pain has an echo: it is called love.

Cadmus

Then the old king will honor what the young king denies—

Pentheus

This is treason: all will answer.

*Exit Pentheus.*

Ghost

 After the snow. The cinders of the trees quivered in
 blue.

Cadmus

 Our position is the only ground we cannot map; our
 fate is the only one that doesn't spell itself out in the
 pool of stars...

Tiresias

 Good health and a willingness to dance: that is all the
 God asks of us...His wrath will stun Pentheus.

Ghost

 The black night flower. The blackened violet of the
 rain.

Cadmus

 My house will be razed—

Raving Ones

 The petals of pale violets, pressed over the eyelids of
 the dead.

Tiresias

 Let's go into the hills. We will end our days dancing.

Cadmus

 We will lean on each other. Two old men falling
 would be an ugly thing.

 *They exit.*

Ghost

Repair yourself to love. Extract the spring from its shell. Run out into the storm. Breath freely through language again. Skip this tragedy like a pebble across a stream.

Raving Ones

The God will punish Pentheus. Pentheus will become a lament. A word for 'grief'.

Ghost

We are all creatures of shame.

Raving Ones

The torn fragments of the sun. We awake like children in this luminousness.

Ghost

There is more pain than beauty in him. White like the dead, almost Etruscan moon. My son.

Raving Ones

That we were the seeds inside of flowers. Children by the sea. Nothing. Nothing. That we were nothing.

Ghost

His name—

Raving Ones

Speak us into motion. Breath past us. Into light.

Ghost

Stripped bare. Abolished. O. This grace. This Godliness. This flood.

Raving Ones

Rising over our shoulders. Like an ocean.

Ghost

The graces, the spirits of longing. The sacred places. I remember them all.

Raving Ones

A pearl of grief—

Ghost

Buried. Drowned.

Raving Ones

My beloved. I don't even know what songs would please you.

Ghost

Perhaps the same bird echoed through both of us yesterday, separate, in the evening.

Raving Ones

Echoing us.

# SCENE 1.2

*Enter Acteon and Heimon.*

Heimon

The earth sleeps.

Acteon

I see lightning in the hills.

Heimon

Thebes is like a ship at sea, with a storm on the horizon.

Acteon

Chaos—

Heimon

Is he the son of Zeus?

Acteon

If Zeus destroyed his own father, he would not want a son.

Heimon

Chaos—

Acteon

I fear them both. I fear all the Gods.

Heimon

Pentheus will lead us into those hills—

Acteon
  Like hunting game—

Heimon
  They will let us chase them, laughing—

Acteon
  They are already laughing.

Heimon
  The soul of nature is an empty shell; the husk of heaven's flower.

Acteon
  No, the human is a shell. Nature is the sea around.

Heimon
  I fear what impiety will mean.

Acteon
  It will be a noise which rings inside this hollow place.

Heimon
  We must find this priest of Dionysus.

Acteon
  We will be the instruments of reason.

Heimon
  We have no other fate.

Acteon
  We must scout into this realm of silence: this realm which cannot be the earth.

Heimon

This is what fear does...it makes the senses wild.

Acteon

There is no Thebes either—

Heimon

This silence dances, like sunlight on the sea.

Acteon

I fear it more than the music.

*Heimon and Acteon exit.*

Ghost

Vast, here, and starry and soft with winds. His hands.
His night. His sky. No. His loss. His wonder.

Raving Ones

Alien.

Ghost

The human has no face.

Raving Ones

Alien.

Ghost

Waters infinitely full of life. Shifting with the moon.

Raving Ones

Alien.

Ghost

A prayer. His music.

Raving Ones
  Alien.

Ghost
  Speaking with an awareness gained through the evolution of suffering.

Raving Ones
  Alien.

Ghost
  A rain cloud hovering over the shoreline. We were marked for grace.

Raving Ones
  Alien.

# Scene 2

*Enter Pentheus, soldiers, and Dionysus bound at the hands.*

Heimon
Pentheus, at your orders, we have caught the priest of Bacchus. He did not move to escape, but came to us, almost willingly, like a doe—

Pentheus
And the Bacchae?

Raving Ones
The Moon with its throat cut. Naked bodies you bent over a fire. Love without softness.

Acteon
They slipped through our net like birds; flew back into the wilderness.

Pentheus
Unbind his hands.

Acteon
His hands are already unbound...

Pentheus
Then bind them again.

Dionysus
Don't be so nervous.

Pentheus

Tell me: why do you practice your rituals in Thebes?
Why do you instigate this madness in our women?

Dionysus

My dreams are too extraordinary not to be shared.

Pentheus

Answer me—

Dionysus

The point of life is to keep one's love alive, so that is
what I do.

Pentheus

And what do you love?

Dionysus

This universe which is insistent on beauty—

Pentheus

What universe?

Dionysus

The universe that howls, shouts, growls, sings, dances.

Pentheus

This is not a human universe.

Dionysus

No universe is human.

Pentheus

You will be punished for your sophistries.

Dionysus
  You will be punished for your faithlessness.

Pentheus
  By whom?

Dionysus
  Dionysus.

Pentheus
  Dionysus is just a name—

Dionysus
  But names are signs—

Pentheus
  Signs of what?

Dionysus
  The polyphonic melody of creation.

Pentheus
  I hear nothing.

Dionysus
  It is a song, a simple song.

Pentheus
  What are you doing in Thebes? Tell me—

Dionysus
  Attempting to alter eternity, like bending a stalk of
  corn between one's hands.

Pentheus
I'll have you buried alive—

Dionysus
I'm buried in divinity already.

*Pentheus doesn't respond.*

Dionysus
What are you afraid of?

Pentheus
How was your God born?

Dionysus
By Semele, your mother's sister.

Pentheus
That is too human a way to be born—

Dionysus
It is not human enough.

*Pentheus doesn't respond.*

Dionysus
Do you hear the wind is rising out of the dark, repeating a phrase from the previous universe: it is telling you to surrender—

Pentheus
Surrender to what?

Dionysus
The chaos of love.

Pentheus

I will cut your hair—

Dionysus

You will not bring the Bacchae back by cutting my hair.

Pentheus

How will I bring them back then?

Dionysus

By joining them.

Pentheus

Then I would not be a king.

Dionysus

You have never been a king.

Pentheus

I am a king in Thebes.

Dionysus

You are just a fish in the mouth of horror.

*Pentheus shears the locks of Dionysus impulsively.*

Pentheus

Order is sacred—

Dionysus

You just broke the heart of the stars.

Pentheus

The stars do not intervene in Thebes.

Dionysus

The children of night are as clever as children of the day.

Pentheus

You will see—Heimon, Acteon: lead the priest to a prison. Charge him through with darkness.

Dionysus

Darkness has solemnity.

*The soldiers lead Dionysus off-stage.*

Pentheus

I could slit the belly of the earth and lay down in the grieving womb. I am cradled helplessly in this clear cosmos. And the moon is an eyelid which opens on me.

*Exit Pentheus.*

*The stage goes dark.*

Ghost

Hew away meaning to find the meaning. Speak.

Raving Ones

Lying at the navel of the earth: unwrinkled like a child.

Ghost

The most beautiful intuition. Alone.

Raving Ones

Each of us, so lovely in our dying. Each of us, dying in our loveliness. In the rain we make a bed of flowers. And we think of ourselves as children, dreaming.

Ghost

Gently, I will remember the tragedy of love.

Raving Ones

Primal grief. Where is our God? We pray. With our eyes closed and our hands pressed to the sun.

Ghost

The enchanter tells his spirits to obey. The sky changes colors. The sea surges up, plucks down the walls of sadness.

Raving Ones

Where has he gone?

Dionysus

*(offstage)* O Bacchae! Hear me! O my Bacchae!

Ghost

The memory of white, unblossomed trees…Death: unbared in all of its loneliness.

Dionysus

And as you said, my poor roses, so beautiful upon the mountain, you "are not worthy of pity". You do not understand yourselves: your fragility, your contempt, your anger. Nature says: grow towards the light like flowers. The Gods say: your fragility is your gift. This, too, is the meaning of my music; my music which says: the human is dying, it is giving way. And when the music decomposes, only the bones of the poem will be left. You must bury them. You must take the remnants of the language in your hands, place it back in the red clay of this, your Theban earth...Do you know who you really are?

# Scene 2.1

*Enter Dionysus above the palace.*

Raving Ones
  The circle is a code the body speaks. We form it, it
  forms us.

Dionysus
  Everything must be connected with life.

Raving Ones
  They've hidden you.

Dionysus
  I was already hidden.

Raving Ones
  Show us your true face.

Dionysus
  Thunder turns consciousness back into nature.

Raving Ones
  Show us.

Dionysus
  Art is the ritual destruction of consciousness.

Ghost/ Raving Ones
  Alien.

Dionysus
  Walk inside yourself and meet no one for hours.

Raving Ones
  Pull down the curtain of the stars.

Dionysus
  Be close to the world. To the trees and the wind that moves through the all things.

Ghost
  He destroyed the palace of Thebes while Pentheus was sleeping. I ran free through the hills and rejoiced.

Dionysus
  My music is the image of thunder. This noise becomes light.

# SCENE 3

*The palace is ruined.*

*Enter Pentheus, soldiers, in pursuit of Dionysus.*

Pentheus
This is too much, Priest—the destruction of the Palace, the House of Cadmus—

Dionysus
I told you someone would free me—

Pentheus
Someone?

Dionysus
My sweet, violent God.

Pentheus
All Gods are sweet and violent.

Dionysus
This God is the most extreme.

Pentheus
The Gods are all limited by fate.

Dionysus
What delimits the Fates then?

Pentheus
I don't know.

Dionysus
The death of the cosmos.

Pentheus
This ruin opens its mouth: it wants to speak. How did you escape? Tell me again—

Dionysus
Your words are as fragile as fish bone—

Pentheus
Tell me.

Dionysus
I willed it.

Pentheus
You mean: you prayed—

Dionysus
No, I willed it.

Pentheus
I feel suspended—

Dionysus
Between?

Pentheus
Exultation and horror.

Dionysus
Don't look down.

Pentheus
What is your trick?

Dionysus
Divinity.

Pentheus
  Divinity is not a trick.

Dionysus
  True. Divinity is thunder.

Pentheus
  Yet you escaped—

Dionysus
  You noticed—

Pentheus
  You could not have escaped.

Dionysus
  You mean: a human could not have escaped.

Pentheus
  Yes.

Dionysus
  One often makes a remark and only later sees how true it is...

  *Pentheus does not respond.*

Dionysus
  Make sure that your religion is a matter between you and your God only—

  *Enter Lykos, a shepherd.*

Pentheus
  Who are you?—

Lykos
Lykos, a humble shepherd. I have come from Mount
Cithaeron, where the Bacchae dance, mad as birds in
a plague.

Pentheus
And?—

Lykos
I fear your temper, Master.

Pentheus
You have my entire impunity—

Lykos
The Bacchae sleep naked like animals. They are
capable of miracles. They brush the ground with
their fingertips and milk wells up from the soil. They
strike their staffs against a stone and wine begins to
leak along the sides. When they dance, the sky turns
bright purple and orange. They suckle wolf cubs and
carry snakes around their waists. At night, they slip
naked into each other's arms—

Pentheus
Is my mother among them?

Lykos
I have seen Agave. She leads them like a general into
battle. They pillage towns, slaughter animals with
their bare hands, cut down trees for great bonfires in
the hills—

Ghost

I knew no other joy.

Lykos

And when the rain falls in the mountains, they run out naked, singing, the mist rising around them; and they look like Gods themselves—

Pentheus

They are just women: our mothers, our daughters, our wives.

Dionysus

The wine unstructures them: they are more like elements.

Pentheus

Shut up. Speak shepherd—

Lykos

They are ordinary...as you say—and yet: their skin has a pearl-like aura...

Pentheus

You lust after them—

Lykos

Master, I—

Pentheus

Do not try to justify yourself. You cannot control yourself.

Lykos

But I have come to warn you—

Pentheus

Then learn to comport yourself properly. You are not in the hills, among your animals—

Dionysus

You are being unfair to him—

Pentheus

He sympathizes with you, priest, though he will not say it.

Dionysus

He is too humble to have sympathy.

Lykos

I have come to warn Thebes. I know my duty. There are fires in the hills, those who do not join the Bacchae are afraid that they will be killed. I can say no more.

Pentheus

Then I cannot hesitate. I will lead a military force into the mountains. You can go shepherd. You must watch your flock.

*Exit Lykos*

Dionysus

I advise you not to take up arms against a God.

Ghost

There are still more beautiful ways of saying 'silence'.

Pentheus

A God has taken up arms against me.

Ghost

The heaviness of the dark blue summer rain, the heavy humidness of the rose-water rain. And the sea in the distance.

Dionysus

A God sings within you, there is a difference.

Pentheus

I'll sacrifice the Bacchae to their God then.

Dionysus

Their God would not like that. Let me bring them back to the city, peacefully.

Pentheus

They would be a contagion then, within the walls.

Dionysus

A man with no appetite despises a well-made meal.

Pentheus

I don't understand.

Dionysus

You look unwell…

Pentheus

I can imagine them propped against each other, back to back, while they sleep; their teeth stained with wine; animal organs scattered around them like fallen leaves. I see my mother in the shape of a serpent with polished skin.

Dionysus

If you try to go to battle against them, you will annihilated. You and all your men.

Pentheus

Then we would die defending Thebes.

Dionysus

You would die disgracing Thebes.

Pentheus

Their strength is exaggerated—

Dionysus

What cannot be imagined cannot be said.

Pentheus

I won't be tricked by you.

Dionysus

Every man is born as many men and dies as a single one.

Pentheus

You don't want your followers destroyed—

Dionysus
  Fool.

Pentheus
  What would you have me do?

Dionysus
  I could disguise you as one of the Bacchae, so that you
  might observe them for yourself.

Pentheus
  I would not be reduced to spying among the hills like
  a bird—

Dionysus
  No no, it will be easy.

Pentheus
  I don't know…

Dionysus
  I will find a fawn-skin for you and a wig. You will
  make the ideal Bacchant.

Pentheus
  I…

Dionysus
  Your skin is still fair, almost like a girl's—

Pentheus
  I'm being tricked—

Dionysus
  And those who were seen dancing were thought to be
  insane by those who could not hear the music...

Pentheus
  What?

Dionysus
  There are no facts, only interpretations.

Pentheus
  How did you escape?

Dionysus
  That is a secret for the initiated.

Pentheus
  Please—

Dionysus
  It would be impossible for you to understand.

Pentheus
  Understand what?

Dionysus
  Without music, life would be a mistake.

Ghost
  A continual self-sacrifice.

Pentheus
  I don't want riddles.

Dionysus
    When night asks who I am I answer, I am yours.

Pentheus
    I don't understand.

Dionysus
    Then let me take you to the Bacchae.

Pentheus
    I can't...

Dionysus
    Where does this urge for truth come from?

Pentheus
    Don't make me answer these questions...

Dionysus
    You're acting like a child—

Pentheus
    You have a power over me...

Ghost
    The texture of the past is like water to you—

Raving Ones
    You've tried your whole life to love what has been
    given to you; but always, you are human.

Dionysus
    You would understand if you wanted to—

Ghost
  The beliefs that crumble into a universe.

Pentheus
  All the pain is there from the beginning. Being born
  just unpacks the sensation—

Raving Ones
  Life is hardly ever real except in dreams. Or in the
  violence of dying for love.

Dionysus
  There are only necessities: there is nobody who
  commands, nobody who obeys, nobody who
  trespasses. If you want something, choose it—

Pentheus
  Everything that deceives enchants…

Dionysus
  One does not kill by anger but by laughter.

Pentheus
  Then why am I so afraid?

Dionysus
  Because you're seeing what you really are.

Pentheus
  And what is that?

Dionysus
  Just look, look—

Ghost

But it's slipped through the black ooze of memory, and it's sinking faster than you can swim down and hug it.

Pentheus

Will they recognize me?

Dionysus

Will you recognize yourself?

Pentheus

I don't know.

Raving Ones

Our nakedness is just a reminder of what we have born between us. Rivers in the trees. The night like oil. The sex we've laid along a darkened sphere. We are like minnows hooked roughly up into the world, while orchids laugh and spirits flap their awful wings.

*Pentheus and Dionysus exit.*

Raving Ones

Our white, bare feet. Our dresses, the color of the moon.

Ghost

He was lead like a fawn into a clearing. Pierced through with darkness.

Raving Ones

It is snowing underneath the world, where the dead gather.

Ghost

The Gods are hunters. We are the fawns—leaping into their nets.

Raving Ones

Rupture. Formless. Half our work is complete.

Ghost

Sweet in the mountains. A cry full of lightning.

Raving Ones

This joy. Come, O Bacchus. We will adore you.

Ghost

Flutes. Calf-skin. Wandering through the mountains, our eyes turned towards the sky. A slate-grey bag, full of the melodies of dying worlds. The music of small things; an anguish, turned into sorrow...

Raving Ones

Milkwhite. They shout. The heavens.

Ghost

Throng. Outrun. Lifted.

Raving Ones

Our silvery nakedness. Gently, rhythmically. The depth of this encounter. Our bodies kissed.

Ghost

Luminous noise.

# SCENE 3.1

*Enter Heimon and Acteon*

Heimon

We cannot die of chaos: we can only pass through it.

Acteon

Order is a symptom of chaos…We are outside the ring of Thebes.

Heimon

Now we are too far. He who dies here does not die by chance.

Acteon

In a dream, one may only speak to oneself.

Heimon

Death is a pure language—

Acteon

Almost like joy—

Heimon

We are being hunted…

Acteon

We are in the country of ritual—

Heimon

The ruins of the mountains. Mocked with echoes.

Acteon
  This is madness, turned into words.

Heimon
  We are inside the myth of ourselves. We are no one.

Acteon
  But we are here.

Heimon
  Will we die?

Acteon
  No.

Heimon
  I think we will die.

Acteon
  No. This is something other than death.

Heimon
  What is it then?

Acteon
  We will discover it.

  *They exit.*

# Scene 4

*Enter Dionysus and Pentheus, in drag, and in a
passive trance.*

Dionysus

I am always working from within tragedy, working
against it, orienting myself to the concept of tragedy,
which is the concept of plurality, plurality of voice,
multivocality inside the spirit of nature. The plurality
of goatsong. Tragedy is consciousness itself: it is
wonder and revelation. Tragedy contains a pre-
awareness of loss, it is pre-emptive mourning. And
consciousness is like the saltwater that fills up and
curves around the spiral in a conch-shell, mimicking
the pattern-spiral without realizing it, and only for a
single, brief exhalation of the waves...

Pentheus

*(entranced)* All emotions are pure which gather in us
and lift us up. They gather in me now.

Ghost

So we are grasped by what we cannot grasp; it has its
inner light, even from a distance—

Pentheus

The side of life which is turned away from us.

Ghost

Just able to endure. He would be consumed.

Raving Ones
  He is the shepherd of Being.

Dionysus
  I am collecting pollens, passing from flower to flower;
  letting myself really feel the pain of enchantment and
  disavowal.

Pentheus
  A voice says: obey the great mystery of grief. You
  grow there, you grow within grief like a single seed.

Ghost
  I bend the willow's branches back. I see what is
  forbidden.

Pentheus
  The experience of the creator is feminine: receiving
  and bearing. This is what I have not allowed myself
  to see until now.

Dionysus
  The body breaks along the lines of its own despair.

Raving Ones
  Drunk on sunlight.

Ghost
  Elderflowers at dusk and the dreams of my child as
  he died.

Dionysus
  Art is recursive: it is always reflecting on itself. Think

about how the world feels when music rushes into the vacuum created by terror: that is what I'm asking you to do. There are things that cannot be put into words. They make themselves manifest. They are what is mystical. The stage is a program for language enacted through silence, gesture, touch.

Pentheus

This difficult solitude. This difficult acceptance.

Dionysus

You stare into the tarnished pools of the sky, and the dense curvatures of time and space that you see there. It is just a pattern that your longing takes.

Ghost

This is my dowery of light.

Pentheus

Life was beautiful then, like lilies stirring in a pond. Something that birds dream of. Space weaves itself into music...

Dionysus

Every ripple of sunlight in the water is a dream you've never had.

Pentheus

I peel away my lips, I impoverish myself before you like a star.

Dionysus

Grace is something you've taken from the House of Despair.

Ghost

No. No. This childlike opening and peeling back of the fragrance of time…The stars that awaken in you and perish in your heart.

Dionysus

Listen closely. It is love that formed me, and that I have learned from. It is love that I build my language out of like a house of stones and mud. And how beautiful people are; I have always felt that: that we are beautifully inexpressible to one another for a reason…

Ghost

The intimacy is noiseless when it isn't there.

Dionysus

I fell through Thebes like rain.

Pentheus

I have never been aware before how many faces there are. Of how much is unrevealed.

Ghost

We found the boy cowering like an animal. Terrified.

Raving Ones

You heard the speech the stars refused. You said that blood is not a sacrifice but an art.

Ghost
  The noise of nothing surrounds you like a bell.

Raving Ones
  The wounds of inspiration have healed in your hands.
  You've learned to mimic the repetition of unconscious
  things.

Pentheus
  What is happening?

Dionysus
  The stage presents itself as a metaphor.

Pentheus
  For what?

Dionysus
  Everything outside of the metaphor.

Pentheus
  Explain to me—

Dionysus
  You cannot hunt the nature out of nature—

Pentheus
  Am I alone here?

Dionysus
  A king is never alone. He is at the center of the hive.
  Surrounded. Fixed into the crystalline structure of
  human order.

Pentheus
  Should I feel ashamed?

Dionysus
  What is there to be ashamed of?

Pentheus
  Joy.

Raving Ones
  I will crush the parasite under my heel.

Dionysus
  What did you expect to find on Mount Cithaeron
  other than the snake that twists around the trunk of
  divinity?

Pentheus
  Joy.

Dionysus
  And what do you want now?

Pentheus
  To be destroyed.

Dionysus
  Two eternities are before you: one with more magic
  in it than the other. Sacred world: this is the intimate
  tragedy of art; of the universe uncreating itself; of
  the stars folding back into their boxes. Sacred world,
  magic lantern show. Hear me! Because everything

depends on this perspective: the perspective of the artist who wants to lose his fear. Wake up!

*Dionysus kisses Pentheus.*

*Pentheus awakens.*

*Exit Dionysus.*

Pentheus

I dreamt that I was pulled apart like a chain of daisies, that my blood was used to fertilize the sun. I dreamt that I found the Bacchae in a meadow, their hair undone, their breasts bared. As I watched them, they turned and watched me. My disguise hadn't worked. But it was not meant to work, it was never meant to work. And I knew then, that my life was over. When the Gods send us dreams, they reveal our fate. I was never a king, I was a lamb: raised and fattened for sacrifice.

Ghost

Deeper than memory. I did not see my son. He was not beautiful to me. This life cannot be griefless. We destroy what we love. I heard the flutes of divinity within me. So I danced and danced.

*The Raving Ones form a tight circle around Pentheus so that Pentheus cannot be seen.*

*Pentheus re-emerges slowly from the center of the circle, like a seedling from underground, and is carried offstage by The Raving Ones.*

# Scene 5

*Enter Heimon and Acteon.*

Acteon
  Thebes is desolate.

Heimon
  The liturgy of the air says that the Gods have fled,
  that we are alone.

Acteon
  Do not forget where we are.

Heimon
  Where are we?

Acteon
  I've forgotten already.

  *Enter Tiresias and Cadmus.*

Cadmus
  Soldiers of Thebes, where is the King?

Heimon
  We're unsure.

Tiresias
  The point of the ritual is to forget.

Acteon
  What ritual?

Tiresias
The ritual of the Bacchae.

Heimon
The Bacchae! We were following the Bacchae! But we did not find them.

Tiresias
No, but they found you.

Acteon
How do you know?

Cadmus
We watched them watching you. We have been in the hills for days, drinking and performing the dances of the God—

Heimon
What God?

Cadmus
Dionysus.

Acteon
That name...

Tiresias
You perform the ritual very well—

Acteon
What ritual?

Tiresias
  Erasure.

Acteon
  What has been erased?

Tiresias
  Names and laws.

Heimon
  Why do you still know then, the names of things?

Tiresias
  My friend and I believed in the God too late, we are
  punished with lucidity.

Heimon
  Who is your friend?

Cadmus
  I am Cadmus; I was once King in Thebes.

Acteon
  What is Thebes?

Tiresias
  Thebes is a secret.

Heimon
  What is the secret?

Tiresias
  That secrecy is a place where meaning is enclosed.

Heimon
  Is that place Thebes?

Tiresias
  The Gods, after the fire of creation, threw away the
  ash from the hearth pan. It was from those ashes that
  the human was born.

Heimon
  Why are you weeping?

Tiresias
  Because I have looked into the eyes of sacrifice.

Acteon
  But you are blind—

Tiresias
  Not within.

Heimon
  Tell us: where should we go? Thebes is empty.

Cadmus
  What the God empties, he will fill again.

Acteon
  How do you know?

Cadmus
  Because the God must always have something to
  destroy.

Heimon
  Who is the God?

Cadmus
  Dionysus.

Acteon
  It is so easy to forget.

    *The sound of thunder.*

Tiresias
  Something terrible…

Heimon
  What?

Cadmus
  A death.

Acteon
  The sky is split.

Heimon
  We must leave here.

Cadmus
  We will stay here.

Acteon
  You will perish—

Tiresias
  There are no rules.

Heimon
    There is only terror.

    *Acteon and Heimon exit, fleeing.*

Cadmus
    Why does the imbalance between the divine and the
    human have to be corrected with a killing?

Tiresias
    In order to purify.

Cadmus
    But what must be purified?

Tiresias
    Pleasure.

Cadmus
    We should return to Thebes, Tiresias. We only
    embarrass ourselves.

Tiresias
    Each step only takes us further into the ritual. It does
    not matter which direction we go.

    *They exit.*

# Scene 5.2

*Enter The Raving Ones, covered in blood.*

Raving Ones

Eyes will trace, review reveal. Eyes will wander like stone-gatherers along the shore. Eyes will grow like an animal at the back of a cave.

Ghost

It's just the way his shoulders collapsed in my hands...

Raving Ones

Stay behind, among the echoes, to make a clean new music.

Ghost

Characterized by an unsuffering kind of faith, not unlike love.

Raving Ones

Speech older and more objective than any words of reason. It is unconcealed, like intimacy.

Ghost

The body after death separating like oil from water. This enclosure of heart and hands. I said I'd outgrow you. You said I'd outgrow you...Love is the re-enchantment of the world.

Raving Ones

Touch will sacrifice itself again. Touch will draw you back to noise.

*Re-enter Tiresias and Cadmus.*

Raving Ones

Describe to me the darkness as it sits on its haunches like a beast and bays at the moon. Describe to me the imagery jointed together in the sun.

Ghost

We disclose ourselves to the stars.

Cadmus

I sowed horror in the ground of Thebes. Now that horror flowers and bears fruit—

Tiresias

The fruit which Dionysus picks and feeds to his followers—

Cadmus

Pentheus...

Tiresias

There is a structure inside of death that resembles life—

Cadmus

Herdsmen bring the torn parts of his body back, one by one—unsure of how to bury their king.

Tiresias

This is the promised end.

Cadmus

Semele's child...

Tiresias

A child of impossible things—

Cadmus

Halfhuman.

Tiresias

No, nature itself.

Cadmus

Pentheus was the last of my line.

Tiresias

We cannot build on the ground of the future, it shakes whenever a God laughs or sings.

Cadmus

They are like messages from another world, the broken letters of his body—

Tiresias

Yet the Bacchae carry no message.

Ghost

And around the edges of darkness there is only silence. A longing sewn into the blood of your prayers. Each day is a failure to speak what is inside of you.

Cadmus

They are themselves the message I think: they are themselves the language which Dionysus speaks. Their dance, their song, their violence: all carry the mark of his voice.

Tiresias

They are a poem then. A single, static image.

Cadmus

Where are we?

Tiresias

Thebes.

Cadmus

I cannot recognize it.

Tiresias

What do you see?

Cadmus

Nothing.

Tiresias

Are you blind?

Cadmus

No: I see too much.

Tiresias

That is a kind of blindness.

Ghost

We make the sacred out of our teeth, our hair, our
breasts, our hands, our sex. The sky is delicate and
full of angels. In every moment we are alive with the
dead.

Raving Ones
    It is like a changeling: the fire in you. The others it
    sought, the enchantments it let be ground into dust.

Cadmus
    Thee raving ones have torn my house up by the
    roots...

Tiresias
    This is all that time is—

Cadmus
    It was my daughter who bore this strange, shattering
    God...

Raving Ones
    The future has consumed itself.

Ghost
    The strangeness culls itself together in your lungs. It
    cries itself from the bottom of a lake.

Tiresias
    Time has disappeared, the future is ecstatic...

Cadmus
    By next winter I will be a flower, nested underneath
    the snow, my eyelids cut off with a paper knife.

Raving Ones
    So that you may never sleep.

Tiresias
    You have seen too much already—

Cadmus

They say Agave lead the Bacchae in the slaughter of Pentheus.

Tiresias

The mystical is not how the world is, but that it is.

Ghost

You know that you are running out of words. That soon you will be left with the choral music you hear in the sun.

Cadmus

I did not believe even a God was capable of such cruelty.

Ghost

Always, when you die, you pray for pity and some peace. The nights brushed with snow, the days cut with thunder.

Raving Ones

Moonlight and mud. The grass between our teeth.

Tiresias

A sadist is always at the same time a masochist...

Cadmus

Tell me: what can the old look forward to?

Ghost

Revelation. Disintegration.

Tiresias

The wayfarer might gain courage through whistling in the dark, but he does not see any more clearly for doing so.

Ghost

You can't hear the cognitive music, can you? The chords are hushed in the hollows of the moon-like words.

Cadmus

I cannot bear to see his whole body assembled.

Tiresias

The head has not been brought back to Thebes.

Cadmus

Let it remain out in the dark.

Raving Ones

And the echo of this music is like a child in you, or a flower.

Ghost

The hoops of darkness open up before you wide and the teeth are like angels.

Tiresias

Surely Dionysus will wish for Thebes to look into its own eyes.

*Cadmus is silent.*

Tiresias

Surely—

Ghost
  You beside me, but no longer. And the music of the
  as-before, so half-remembered.

Cadmus
  It was my daughter who bore him...

Tiresias
  She died.

Cadmus
  He lived. Dionysus lived.

Ghost
  We find the uncreated here: underneath whatever
  defines itself as grace.

Tiresias
  The ruins of a life are always incomplete, enigmatic,
  never entirely intelligible, like any system of the
  divine.

  *They exit.*

Raving Ones
  Dionysus, magician, director. The clearness of you,
  the terrible clinging of our bodies to the air. Forbids
  me. So much physical haunting pleasure. So much so.

Ghost
  The prayer of death divined within itself.

Raving Ones
  We join our meditations with the sun. Wash the lame

feet of our salvation. O. The breaking out of the petal-shells into color.

Ghost

Tell me the rain is a creation of love. Tell me that love is the creation of your voice.

Raving Ones

A boy hushed in the rain. Like an animal. We recognized the young king. We tore him limb from limb.

Ghost

I touch the sunlight sealed in the trees—

Raving Ones

We go down to the River of Silence and draw up the God Bacchus by his soft feet. We pray that this is the God of our hearts. The only God who is the God of life.

Ghost

My son...

Raving Ones

Hushed in the trembling voices of birds. Dionysus. Sing!

Ghost

Of the silent you are the most gentle—

Raving Ones

We must sing ourselves to sleep.

# Scene 6

*Enter Agave, holding the head of Pentheus, trailed by Bacchae.*

Ghost

Time and memory are like two olive trees, grown slowly together...

Raving Ones

It was you.

Agave

Not with hunting nets, but with our soft white hands. Where is my old father?—Let him come. Where is my son Pentheus?—Let him see that I have caught a lion.

Ghost

I always said, I will wait for you, beneath the trees of ash.

*Enter Cadmus and attendants, bearing the litter with the rest of Pentheus's body.*

Cadmus

The servants of Thebes have pieced together the ruins of its King. Do you recognize what you have done?

Ghost

Black loneliness. The moon with its arms flung around the stars, fingers spread.

Agave
  No.

Cadmus
  O, immeasurable grief. Sheer butchery…sheer butchery.

Agave
  What reason is there for grief?

Cadmus
  You hold it—

Agave
  I hold the head of a lion. Will you not recognize the bravery of your daughter?

Cadmus
  I am too occupied with mourning.

Agave
  Mourning for what?

Ghost
  I remember less and less about myself: I am evolving into a creature outside of time.

Agave
  I do not need to see except as the God sees.

Cadmus
  Then you cannot see the God's fury.

Agave

I see the head of a lion.

Cadmus

The calligraphy of death is written on its skin.

Agave

Father, you must praise what the God has done through me.

Cadmus

The God has mocked you—

Agave

He is covert, implicit, unverbalized: he is what the human form bends to.

Cadmus

I know the God. I have gone into the mountains and performed his rituals. I have tried to dream my way back into his grace. But it was not enough. It could not be enough. I lie awake in this darkness now.

Ghost

The syntax must twist around and look at itself.

Raving Ones

You must learn how to speak the language of people who have lost their hope.

Ghost

Grief as low as a syllable.

Agave
  Father, Thebes knows his favor. It is all around us—

Cadmus
  I smell the ruined body—

Agave
  Do not blanch at what is holy.

Cadmus
  Dionysus punished you, Agave. He put a madness
  into you. You were impious.

Ghost
  The transition that occurs when one remains silent.

Cadmus
  My child, look.

Agave
  And suddenly: this feeling of having woken up at the
  bottom of a lake in winter.

  *Agave drops the head.*

Agave & Ghost
  My beautiful child.

Raving Ones
  The wind in your hair, pieces of broken moonlight
  flying by.

Ghost

Remembering my whole life in a. O. My love, yes, my.

Raving Ones

Body giving way to form. Free, then the body's gone.

Agave

The chords of my throat, tight. Like a valve. No more singing.

Raving Ones

Through a screen of resistance. A force turns us out of life like orphans.

Cadmus

Ringing in my ears, I'll swim through it. Reach back to her—

Ghost

When in the evening, the sun through the wheat. Shrieking, mad with. My body of oak and granite. My. Sun crowning all. At night we. Reclaims us, the blackness. My father's country in the dusk, my hands between the wheat stalks—

Agave

Alien.

Ghost

In an unpeopled world, all will live. Soon. Our bodies stripped to nothing.

Raving Ones

Blue, that star-shower. His hair, his mouth. All that we embrace. The God—

Ghost

My spiritual body, rotting like an uncored apple.

Raving Ones

White moon. Her eyes white, turning over.

Cadmus

Some presence seeks us, it will gut us like fish.

Ghost

How far like stems we push through the ground of time. Soon to be reaped like corn.

Agave

My body is a long arc of light, it slips beyond the horizon.

Cadmus

Her body is a dark flower, radiating out from the kernel of the groin.

Raving Ones

The mind driven like cattle towards the end—

Ghost

Like a tree felled at the base, toppling into darkness.

Raving Ones

Dumb among the bodies. A beast broken, howling on its back.

Ghost

Headlands of mourning. I'll face it, no. I'll turn away.

Agave

This is the last stillness before the body unwinds. I am a thread of gossamer.

Ghost

Already silent. The tenor birds poached. Who embodies this grief?

Agave

Me. Sealed within this bleak envelope of mud.

Cadmus

Will anyone who has watched this scene deny that Dionysus is a God?

*Enter Dionysus.*

Dionysus

On our way back from pain we might remember that poems have names, or that you get tragedy where the tree, instead of bending, breaks...Now, my thunder is the silence which breaks out over Thebes... Because for years, I gave away sexual love with my eyes. Now I don't. I don't have a name for what I give away; unsilent prayers, touch without mourning. I remember my first poems like shocks of static electricity. Now, they are like grains of salt dissolved in the geometry of water. This is the lull of my exile: my shadow floating over the stage like the cry of a bell from another life. The preference of time, and the allegory for time (which is tragedy) is to fold itself into a continuous sequence of longing: because the shape of a memory, like a poem, is classical: its beauty is something as ancient as mathematical knowledge; but it, like the memory itself, is also fragile, and unbearably delicate. This speech is my maturity, my acceptance, my last act, and these are the conditions of my art: perpetual remembering, self-understanding without self-transcendence. Because this is what it means to leave the theater and to go home. It means you can drop a bucket into a reservoir of stars and draw up their water. It means that the soul is beautiful, left alone; like a figural drawing of a bellflower; an erasure; another day wasted, smudged, drawn out again. And there is only one way for a soul to flourish: the way through language back to laughter. This is the meaning of my Raving Ones. My projections, my holograms, my myths...A hero looks death in the face, real death, not just the image of death. Behaving honourably in a crisis doesn't mean being able to act the part of a hero well, as in the theatre, it means being able to look death itself in the eye. For an actor may play many roles, but at the end of time, the simple human animal is the one who has to die. This is the punishment I give to you, to Thebes: to die as yourselves, to leave the theater as people and not as myths. We are trying to hide—to hide our innermost selves, this deep, fearful drive to kill everything—and to blend in with everyone else, so no one sees or suspects the destructive Life that we call 'blood'. Is Life purely masculine, killing in order not to die—and using the power of imitation to do so—or is it not, also, feminine, willingly accepting (and seeking?) death in order to truly give birth, to a new—and never-ending—creation. It is both. It must be both. So turn a personal failure into a cosmic tragedy: this is all that tragedy can be now. Because we've forgotten how to ask for it (the rain). How to call it down from the sky. How to dance for it like we feel innocent again. This stage should be like a tree, with its roots in the spring mud; with branches strong enough to hold a climbing child. It is a platform for a play struggling into life: forming itself after its own struggle; a chrysalis of language, merging into One from multiplicity.   Now, by becoming an aesthetic artifact I become human. Now by becoming human, I become divine. Follow me.

www.ingramcontent.com/pod-product-compliance
Lightning Source LLC
LaVergne TN
LVHW041233080426
835508LV00011B/1195